DWELL GATHER BE

DWELL GATHER BE

DESIGN FOR MOMENTS

ALEXANDRA GOVE

BLUE·STAR
PRESS

BLUE·STAR
PRESS

Published by Blue Star Press
PO Box 8835, Bend, OR 97708
contact@bluestarpress.com
www.bluestarpress.com

Photography | Ali Vagnini
(unless otherwise noted below)

Photography on pages 106, 112, 113 | Élan Photographie Studio

Cover Design | Amanda Hudson

Interior Design | Chris Ramirez & Amanda Hudson

ISBN 9781944515607

Printed in China
10 9 8 7 6 5 4 3 2 1

Dedicated to my family

on both sides of the ocean,

for teaching me how to create

a thoughtful home.

CONTENTS

FOREWORD

HOW can we measure happiness? Why are some people happier than others? How can we improve quality of life? These are the questions that we try to solve at the Happiness Research Institute.

The more people I meet and the more conversations I have around happiness, the more I realize that we might be Americans, Dutch, and Danish—but we are first and foremost people. The same things bring happiness in Copenhagen and Colorado.

One of the conversations that taught me this was with Alexandra and her husband Koen in a wine bar in Copenhagen on a cold spring afternoon.

What had brought us all together was hygge. The best short definition of hygge is, "the art of creating a nice atmosphere." It is those moments where we experience togetherness, relaxation, comfort, simple pleasures, and peace of mind. I have tried to describe hygge and understand how it impacts our happiness. Across the Atlantic, Alexandra and Koen have tried to understand how to create hygge in our homes.

Our homes shape our lives. It is where we find relaxation and safety. It is where we let our guards down and connect with our loved ones. Our home is a place to escape to, to be alone, to switch off. We need to understand and harness the impact our homes have on our happiness, as most of us spend more time in our homes than anywhere else.

Meeting Alexandra and Koen gave me a new question to wrestle with: What makes a home a happy one? I think *Dwell, Gather, Be* is part of the answer.

MEIK WIKING
Author of *The Little Book of Hygge: Danish Secrets to Happy Living*

INTRODUCTION

IN 2012, I moved to Amsterdam to be with my boyfriend (now my husband and business partner). I will always remember the day I arrived. I packed lightly for a move of this magnitude, or so I thought, until I saw Koen waiting for me at the airport. He had ridden his bicycle and brought an extra for me. With an easy smile on his face, he biked home with one 50-pound suitcase balanced on the bicycle's rack and the other rolling alongside his bicycle. Luckily, I only had to manage my backpack!

As an American living in Europe for the first time, so many things felt different—and not just bicycling around with luggage in tow! Friendships were somewhat difficult to form. They took time to cultivate but were unwavering once established. European décor is minimal and intentional; homes filled only with things that hold a purpose or special meaning. Real candles burned in cafés—the warm ambience more important than any possible fire hazard. I could linger in those same cafés for as long as I desired, and never feel that I had overstayed my welcome. In fact, to my American eyes, it felt as though the Dutch had mastered the art of lingering over meals. Evenings with family or friends were spent at the dinner table, enjoying multiple courses and absorbed in hours of conversation. What I realized later is that most of these subtle differences I noticed during those first months living abroad were all examples of *gezelligheid*. The Dutch word, *gezellig*—for which there is no direct English translation—is used to describe the coziness and comfort of a particular setting, a person, or a moment. Life in the Netherlands was my first encounter with this northern European way of living intentionally, being present, and slowing down to enjoy everyday moments.

In 2013, I traveled to Copenhagen with a friend in search of Danish design and inspiration. Like in Amsterdam, there were candles everywhere, flickering in windows, and on every café table. Cozy charm was all around, and the people seemed content and happy. In Copenhagen is where I found *hygge*— essentially the Danish equivalent of gezelligheid. At first, I felt hygge. When I learned that a word existed to describe the feeling, sparks flew. It was as if I had found my life match, my calling. I was enchanted with hygge spaces and the special moments and feelings they inspired. I realized that even *things* could generate good feelings. Something as simple as a well-crafted mug might trigger the release of a contented sigh. In Denmark, thoughtful, simple design underpins hygge. I had already fallen in love with a Dutchman, and I now found myself attracted to this northern European lifestyle. When I discovered hygge (and gezelligheid), I realized that everything I admired and loved about these cultures was encapsulated in a single word in each language, a word I could use to refer to the candlelit cafés, to the thoughtful conversation I shared with a friend, and to a cozy home filled with soft textures and intentionally curated décor. As I dug deeper into hygge, I discovered that the Norwegians, Swedes, Germans, and Finns espoused similar lifestyles and that each language has words with similar meaning.

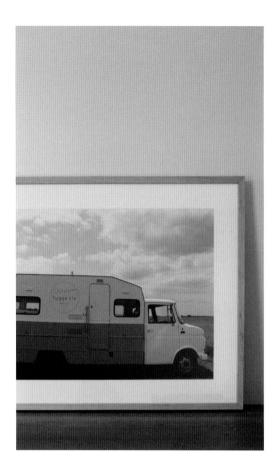

My fascination with this way of living had taken hold and was not easily relinquished. It was this discovery that inspired me to start *Hygge Life*. With a vague desire to spread hygge, Koen and I bought an old 1971 Opel Blitz camper van. We spent several months fixing it up and dubbed it the "Hygge Bus." Young and in love, we began an adventure traveling around Europe that summer, selling *poffertjes* (tiny Dutch pancakes) at markets and campsites. We were both seeking and creating hygge as we made and shared pancakes and sold beautiful textiles from our happy blue bus. Along the way, we expanded our offerings and set up a roving general store that boasted nostalgic candies, toys, and other goodies. We were fully engaged in the experience of sharing hygge with others, capturing our adventure on the *Hygge Life* blog as we traveled.

As our summer travels came to an end, I was determined to continue to share this lifestyle. Since I was most drawn to spaces that emanate coziness and contentment, I began to collect "hygge vintage," with the plan to take these items home to the United States to sell at markets to inspire Americans to create a *hyggelig* atmosphere in their homes. I collected vintage candle holders, woolen blankets, dining accessories, and antique roe deer antlers—items that I associated with special moments and places. After experiencing importing pains and selling my favorite finds from days of flea market digging (with a few broken pieces along the way), I realized that there were many more ways to spread hygge and to continue to build and grow *Hygge Life*.

2016—our first year back in the US—was a whirlwind of activity. Koen and I moved to my home state of Colorado to begin our new life together. I was passionate and excited to share hygge with our American family and friends, confident that this European lifestyle would be embraced and celebrated. Koen and I participated in markets and pop-ups in Colorado and around the rest of the country, sharing our story and collections of European products, while still maintaining the blog and online shop (not to mention planning our wedding!). To our surprise, hygge became a global trend that year. This Danish concept was embraced around the world, and it invited lots of conversation and interest. We loved to see the light in people's eyes as they realized that they *had* hygge in their lives but were never able to express it fully. Hygge gave a means—a word —to be able to recognize and fully appreciate these special moments. The items we sold reinforced the message we were sharing and gave people a visual, physical representation of hygge, a way to begin to intentionally recognize and introduce coziness and moments of connection into their homes and lives.

Soon thereafter, Koen and I moved from Denver to the charming ski town of Vail and opened our *Hygge Life* brick and mortar store. Here, we share and sell home goods collected from our European travels and help people create hyggelig spaces in their homes. From the first day, we have loved welcoming people into our shop and sharing our story. The excitement we see in people when they first learn about hygge continually inspires us. We recently added an adjoining café where we encourage our guests to slow down and experience hygge. Just as I experienced an "aha" moment in Copenhagen years ago, we now watch others awaken to a deeper, more intentional way of living.

Hygge gave a means—a word—to be able to recognize and fully appreciate these special moments.

Witnessing these moments is a constant reminder that in the English language, we don't have a single, all-encompassing word to capture this "all is well" feeling. "Perfection" perhaps hints at it, but these moments aren't always perfect. Sometimes the imperfections of a moment can make it even more special. "Contentment" and "hominess" also come close, as does "coziness." But why doesn't the English lexicon have a similar word? Does it indicate that we don't experience these moments? Certainly not! Does it mean that our culture doesn't intentionally encourage these moments as other cultures around the world do? Possibly.

This "just right" feeling isn't unique to Europe, or Europeans. The moments that we universally treasure bring a feeling of contentment, the sense that there is nowhere else we'd rather be. These moments are big and small, significant and insignificant. The trick is to continually and intentionally cultivate these moments and to take the time to recognize and appreciate them. My time living in Europe taught me that when there is a unified concept for these moments, they are pursued more intentionally, occur more often, and are valued. I don't think it is far-fetched that this recognition and appreciation of life's moments, both big and small, leads to a happier life.

I have always enjoyed making my spaces cozy, from my childhood bedroom to my college dorm room to my first apartment. I am a true homebody. When I first moved to Amsterdam and Koen and I moved into an apartment together, I was eager to dress it up. I would go shopping and bring home random décor. I wasn't necessarily thinking

The moments that we universally treasure bring a feeling of contentment, the sense that there is nowhere else we'd rather be.

14

WORDS FOR MOMENTS

A variety of European languages have words that capture the feeling one has when a moment or atmosphere is just right:

HYGGE (HOO-GA)
DANISH

A sense of wellbeing, coziness, and contentment.

> *Spending a dark winter evening at home with your family, sharing a meal over candlelight, or playing a board game together.*

GEZELLIG (GEZEL-IG)
DUTCH

A convivial and comfortable atmosphere where you feel content and at ease.

> *Drinking beers on a Friday night with friends in a charming, candlelit "brown cafe."*

GEMÜTLICH (GUH-MOOT-LIK)
GERMAN

A feeling of warmth, friendliness, and good cheer.

> *Picnicking in the park with your family and friends on a warm summer day while watching your children run around and play.*

KOSELIG (KOSE-LIG)
NORWEGIAN

A sense of warmth, security, and coziness.

> *Sitting by a roaring fire with friends after a long day of skiing.*

LAGOM (LA-GOM)
SWEDISH

Not too little, not too much, just right.

> *Enjoying a work-life balance and sharing dinner with your family each day.*

MYSIG (MY-SIG)
SWEDISH

Sharing in an activity with others that is comfortable or pleasurable.

> *A Friday evening gathering with friends filled with food, conversation, and relaxation.*

PÄNTSDRUNK (PANTS-DRUNK)
FINNISH

A state of relaxation.

> *Drinking at home in your underwear with no intention of going out.*

15

about the purpose of these items or the quality, but I felt compelled to fill our space. I was surprised by Koen's instinctive, negative reaction. He had difficulty understanding why I would bring meaningless, impractical items into our home. Our different viewpoints led me to a life-changing realization. With a jolt, I recognized my behavior as a cultural habit. In the coming weeks and months as I visited the homes of Koen's family members and those of new friends, I noticed commonalities in their carefully curated yet minimally decorated homes. Each piece therein had a story to tell—a painting inherited from a relative, a custom-made piece of furniture, or another item that someone loved and saved to purchase. Even practical, everyday objects were carefully selected to enhance the daily life of the owner.

Immersed in this new culture, I began to recognize intentional, thoughtful ways to make a home feel homey, ways that took more time but were satisfying and lasting. This gradual realization evolved to a deeper understanding of how to create a hyggelig or gezellig home. A home should accommodate the lifestyles of its inhabitants, and most importantly, each room should thoughtfully be designed to cultivate the special moments that take place within it. A dimly lit living

room with cozy throw blankets and cushions scattered about encourages relaxation and connection; a

You can cultivate profound, even sacred moments in your life beginning in your home— elevating, celebrating, and valuing the time you spend with those you hold most dear in the space that is uniquely yours.

kitchen—so often the busiest room in the house—may be playfully unkempt as it cheerfully fulfills everyone's most basic needs. It isn't about filling a home with trendy or expensive furniture and décor, but rather about things that hold meaning or purpose. Thoughtful homes do not come together overnight. The process of creating a contented abode takes time and consideration.

Back in the United States and readapted to my native culture, I have grown more passionate about cultivating cherished moments in the home. After all, I have experienced the most profound hyggelig moments at home, either in my own home or in the homes of close friends and family. As the American saying goes, "Home is where the heart is." We can cultivate profound, even sacred moments in our lives by beginning in our homes—elevating, celebrating, and valuing the time we spend with those we hold most dear in the space that is uniquely ours.

Our life—mine and Koen's—has evolved organically over the years. We were once young lovers roaming Europe sharing hygge; now we are the owners of a store in a mountain town (and still in love!). But our passion and mission remain the same through the years: to help people discover a more intentional, thoughtful way to experience moments in their lives.

Dwell, Gather, Be explores my interpretation of hygge for our American culture that lacks corresponding terminology. These three facets bring a sense of happiness and fulfillment to our lives. Where we **DWELL** is where we meet our most basic needs: where we nourish ourselves, where we rejuvenate, where we seek comfort, and where we experience a feeling of security and belonging. Home is also where we **GATHER**. Humans are social creatures; we crave connection and are drawn to share our homes, meals, thoughts, and laughter with those we hold dear. However, to feel entirely at peace where we dwell and to find deep fulfillment in our relationships with others, we must also care for ourselves. We must learn to **BE**, to slow down, practice self-care, and to grant ourselves moments of solitude to rejuvenate. Each facet works in tandem. *Dwell, Gather, Be* shares how thoughtful and intentional design creates a home that is uniquely yours, one that allows you to foster deep, satisfying connections with the people you care about and to be present as you cultivate a life you love.

DWELL

DWELL

DWELL

*Create spaces that meet your basic needs
and help you thrive.*

WHEN I lived in Amsterdam, I loved to bike along the *grachtengordel* (the canal ring) in the evening hours. On one side stood a row of tall, slim houses, each one different than the next, and on the other side the water glistened with reflections of the surrounding homes. To the Dutch people, it's a well-known practice of the grachtengordel residents to leave their curtains wide open and the interior lights on during the evening hours. Perhaps they enjoy showing off their coveted homes, or perhaps they appreciate the view of the busy streets below. I like to think that they want to share their homes with the strangers passing by outside,

locals and tourists alike. I loved getting a glimpse into the lives of the people who reside in those beautiful, historic canal houses. And in truth, their lives are fairly ordinary. I would often see a family sitting down for dinner by candlelight, an elderly gentleman in a comfortable chair with a book in hand, or a little girl and her mother standing in the window, peering at the boats floating past. I remember bicycling past a home on the *Prinsengracht* and seeing a multigenerational family gathered around for supper. There was a vase of flowers in the center of the table and everyone was laughing, eating, and having a seemingly

wonderful time. I couldn't help but smile, reminded of similar moments with my own family.

During my Amsterdam years, I became accustomed to this culture of openness. For me, it was a gentle, subtle reminder that we are all doing our best to meet our basic needs while also seeking happiness and contentment, each in our unique ways. Dutch cultural values encourage a general acceptance and transparency in people's lives. So, while the canal ring homes are some of the most sought-after addresses in Europe, practically speaking, these homes serve the same general purpose for their residents. Whether grand or humble, home is home. It's the moments we create and live in our homes—what is visible through the windowpane—that bring us together.

Home. It may be a sprawling, multi-level abode or a studio apartment. It may sit on acreage or in the middle of a bustling city. No matter where home is, we all retreat there to meet our most basic needs. We find shelter and rest. The meals we prepare feed us, and we draw comfort from familiarity and a sense of belonging. Our homes reflect who we are and how we live our lives. However, we may sometimes fail to recognize—or even neglect—the role that home plays in our most fundamental (and arguably most important) life experiences. Or, we may focus purely on aesthetic concerns, on the way our homes look rather than how they feel and influence how we live our daily lives. I believe that a home should be designed to foster and enhance life's special moments, rather than around a trend or a high-end piece of furniture. Design your home to complement your lifestyle and use design as a means to cultivate sacred moments—the moments that ultimately make up your life.

Whether grand or humble, home is home. It's the moments we create and live in our homes—what is visible through the windowpane—that bring us together.

The look of your home—a clutter-free minimalist abode or an exotic, bohemian space bursting with vibrant color—reveals something about you. It reflects your personality, your values, what brings you peace, and what brings you pleasure. Your home doesn't have to look like it belongs in a magazine and it needn't adhere to what's fashionable. Neither makes a home truly home-like, and the struggle for perfection is untenable as trends shift over time. A more fulfilling (and more sustainable) approach is to look inside yourself to discover what truly brings you happiness and to imagine a space that will help you to create these moments of joy. Activity, messes, treasured moments with loved ones—these are what make a home, and a life.

WHERE YOU ARE
NOURISHED

I sometimes daydream about being an Italian *nonna*, a brightly-colored scarf tying back my curly hair, a flour-covered linen apron tied around my hips. I see myself making homemade pasta, preparing a delicious meal for my children and grandchildren to enjoy. Is it strange to look forward to growing old and cooking for my family? There is something deeply satisfying about preparing a homemade meal for my loved ones to take pleasure in. I believe that providing a meal is one of the simplest yet most meaningful ways to show love for others. So far, the closest I've gotten to my kitchen daydream is to cook for friends, since I have many years before I have grandchildren to feed. But, I relish the practice!

THE KITCHEN

At its most basic, the kitchen is a utilitarian space, yet it draws people. Perhaps it has something to do with the simple fact that food— something we all need and enjoy— comes from the kitchen. Maybe it has to do with the comforting ritual of food preparation or the shared experience of mealtime.

In older homes and apartments, kitchens are often cramped and tiny. In modern homes in the United States, kitchens are more likely to be large, open, and airy, envisioned and designed as a gathering space. This evolution came about because we collectively recognize that we

make memories in the kitchen. Large kitchens can be wonderful. To my mother's dismay (and secret delight, I'm sure!), every relative from the youngest to the oldest finds their way to her big, open kitchen as she prepares Christmas dinner. However, I find that small kitchens, with all of their quirks, can be special in their way. My friend, Deana, has a tiny kitchen. She's an accomplished cook, and it's magical to see the dishes that come from such a modest space. The fact that such delicious meals come from a postage stamp of a kitchen make them even more remarkable. Whether big or small, there is something charming about a slightly messy kitchen. The practical

considerations of the space have a way of erasing any pretentiousness. While kitchens are inherently functional rooms, thoughtful design and décor facilitates not only meal preparation, but also moments of joy and meaningful connection.

There are endless opportunities to infuse even the humblest space with beauty. Whenever I visit my friend Meredith's home, I look forward to using her tea kettle and enjoy looking around her kitchen, admiring the pretty pots and pans. Boiling water for tea is so satisfying—the weight of the kettle, how the button clicks when I press it, and the smooth pour of the water—and I enjoy my

tea more than I do anywhere else. Meredith fully embraces the notion that even the most practical tools in the kitchen can be beautiful, too. Select kitchen items that you enjoy using, holding, and seeing—a small way to infuse pleasure into each day.

Tableware

One day several years ago, I was making lunch and mindlessly pulled a chipped, generic plate from the cupboard. I also owned a set of lovely dishes at the time, but somehow, I found myself "saving" these for only special occasions and using ugly old dishes for the everyday. I suddenly realized just how many random plates, mugs, and pieces of

*Every day is
special and should
be treated as such...*

cutlery filled my kitchen cupboards and drawers. A moment of clarity followed this realization: every day is special and should be treated as such, even down to using dishes that I love, a small but meaningful way to nourish my spirit.

Perhaps you have a set of dishes inherited from your great-grandparents, or a vintage set you found on an outing with your best friend. Consider that the dishes you use could be about the meaning and stories they carry, as well as about how they look, bringing layers of richness to the meals you eat from them.

Kitchen Linens

Kitchen linens add layers of texture and beauty. My favorite kitchen towels are natural cotton or linen; they wear well and serve a variety of functions in the kitchen, from drying glassware or mopping up spills to taking a hot baking dish from the oven.

Find an apron that looks just as good hanging on a peg as it does on. This one has roomy pockets to stash favorite recipes.

Cookware

Take care in choosing your cookware and prep tools. Since you use pots, pans, and cooking utensils almost daily, it is worth investing in items that function well, suit your cooking needs, and that you enjoy using.

Cookbooks

Many cookbooks are a visual delight, full of tempting recipes and wonderful photography. Cookbooks are useful, but they are also a pleasure to leaf through. Consider displaying a few of your most treasured cookbooks in your kitchen. If you have ample counter space, a cookbook easel holds your favorite cookbook and prompts you to use the book instead of reaching for a device, encouraging a moment of mindfulness as you plan and prepare a meal.

MIMI THORISSON

FRENCH COUNTRY COOKING

THE WORLD ATLAS OF WINE 7TH EDITION HUGH JOHNSON JANCIS ROBINSON MITCHELL BEAZLEY

ROBERTSON TARTINE BREAD

Magnus Nilsson

The Nordic Cookbook

COPENHAGEN FOOD TRINE HAHNEMANN

Food as Décor

Fresh fruit and vegetables, dried pasta in interesting shapes, or even a loaf of freshly baked bread—food can be as visually pleasing as a bouquet or a piece of artwork. The colors and textures fill a kitchen with vibrancy and a sense of life. Set a beautiful ceramic bowl with fresh fruit on the countertop or in the center of the kitchen table. It looks lovely and encourages healthy snacking. A simple wooden bowl filled with pistachios is one of my go-to hors d'ouevres when we entertain guests. We nearly always keep a fresh loaf of bread on the breadboard and a pot of fresh basil near the kitchen window. Instead of tucking it away in cabinets, display healthy food in the open and enjoy the daily sights, fresh scents, and feelings of abundance.

*Pause in your day
and savor life's
small pleasures.*

A Slow Approach

When I first moved abroad, I was taken aback by the notion of shopping for food daily—not to mention transporting groceries home by bicycle! Growing up in the United States, grocery shopping involved a weekly trip to the supermarket. In Europe, I came to enjoy my daily rounds to collect milk, eggs, meat or fish, and produce. I came to know the people who produced and sold the fresh food we enjoyed.

While there is a benefit to this slow and thoughtful means of acquiring food, it is just as beneficial to take a similar approach to food preparation. Orange juice squeezed with a hand press is far more satisfying than juice from a carton.

The scent of freshly baked bread adds an irresistible aroma to the air and the beautiful wood grain of a breadboard is a lovely and functional piece in any kitchen.

Bring fresh ingredients into your kitchen as often as possible; grow herbs in the windowsill, keep a kitchen garden, or enjoy a weekly trip to the farmers market, all opportunities to pause in your day and savor life's small pleasures.

As you begin to prepare a meal, gather all of the ingredients you will need and carefully wash the produce, a ritual to bring you to a mindful place to embrace and enjoy the cooking process.

Open Shelving

Kitchens often have lovely features to embrace, such as open shelving to display dishes and cookware. Select the items you place on open shelving with care; they should be both useful and attractive. While open shelving does capture dust and may require more cleaning, glass cabinet doors are another option that gives similar effect but keeps maintenance to a minimum.

Counter Space

In large kitchens, the countertops might hold a vase of flowers, a crock of utensils, or even a collection of cookbooks, items to warm the space and give it a feeling of life. Whether your kitchen is large or small, designate an expanse of countertop for meal preparation. A dedicated, clutter-free area ensures that you can prepare food at any time, and it gives the eye a visual rest in an otherwise busy space.

Windows

This beautiful kitchen boasts large windows and stunning mountain views. The room is bathed in natural light in the morning, flooded with cheerful sunshine in the afternoons, and receives a soft sunset glow in the evening hours. Does your kitchen window afford a lovely view or a cheerful slant of the sun at a particular time of day?

MOMENTS
TO SAVOR

I have sweet memories of baking batch after batch of Christmas cookies with my mom each year. We would spend hours decorating each snowflake, candy cane, and gingerbread man with icing and sprinkles. As I reflect, I realize that these were times when we slowed down to savor each other's company, and this is why these moments have endured in my memory with such fondness.

Create the Moment
There is little as exciting for a child than the opportunity to bake cookies with a beloved grown-up. Wearing an apron, getting messy, watching shapes come to life with cookie cutters, and of course, eating the treat at the end! You cannot rush the process with a child involved. Baking with a child is an opportunity to slow down and relish each step: cracking an egg carefully on the edge of a bowl, scooping fluffy flour from a canister, and pressing a cookie cutter gently into the dough. Involve children in baking or cooking from time to time. The mess may grow exponentially, but the precious memories and looks of pride on their faces are well worth the extra cleanup time. This moment has little to do with what is on the menu and everything to do with the time you spend together.

Design the Moment
Children love to teeter atop a stool to reach the countertop and get involved in whatever is going on in the kitchen. Consider tucking a little step stool in the corner, one just for kids to include them in the cooking process. Vintage metal stools are often tucked into the corners of antique stores; you may even have a wooden step stool from your childhood!

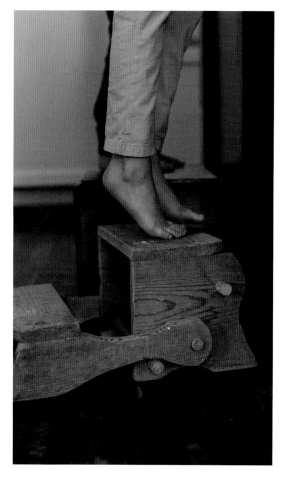

A PLACE TO REST
& REJUVENATE

When we were first married, my husband and I lived for a year in a stunning home tucked into a mountainside just outside of Vail, Colorado. We referred to this as our "honeymoon home." We did not own the house but lived in it as temporary caretakers, a mutually beneficial arrangement with the owner (although we certainly felt we got the best end of the deal)! Early one morning, we both happened to be awake, though we were still in bed. Suddenly a movement outside the enormous bedroom windows caught our attention. A sleek, powerful mountain lion was pacing across the hillside, just yards from our bed. It was a moment of feeling vulnerable in the presence of such a creature, yet entirely safe as we snuggled under the covers.

While this experience is memorable, in truth, I have always thought of my bedroom as a safe haven, a peaceful retreat from the world. Thought and care should guide each detail of bedroom design to create a space that encourages rest and rejuvenation.

53

THE BEDROOM

Home is where we find rest. It is where we wind down after a hectic day and where we sleep to recharge for the next day. Sleep is one of our most fundamental needs and we are healthier, happier, and more productive when we are well-rested. As you design your bedroom, imagine the moments you enjoy in the space and find ways to create a room to enhance your experience. Ultimately, there is nothing quite as comforting as the luxury of coming home each day knowing that there is a warm bed in a cozy bedroom waiting for you.

Create a Calm Environment

Once upon a time, bedrooms were only for sleeping. Nowadays, many people retreat to their beds to watch television, scroll through social media, surf the internet, and even to work. Like so many, I fell into the habit of using my phone as my alarm clock and found myself checking email the moment I opened my eyes in the morning, a pattern that made me feel sluggish, unproductive, and stressed from the moment I awoke.

For a true haven from the outside world, consider eliminating electronics—televisions, phones, and devices of any kind—from your bedroom entirely. An old-fashioned bedside alarm clock will cue you to

go to sleep and wake up on time, and it is an opportunity to add an attractive, unique piece to your bedroom décor. Your sleep will improve, and your mind will benefit from a much-needed respite from the daily onslaught of information. The nature of your mornings will improve, too—you will wake up rejuvenated, happy, and ready for a new day.

To further promote a feeling of calm and to protect the bedroom as a sacred place, commit to keeping it tidy. Functional items may both enhance décor and help keep things in order. A large, attractive basket or bin can capture dirty laundry, or it could be used to hold extra pillows that you remove from the bed at night. A vintage chair near the bed is a place to toss your bathrobe or to keep a spare book or two. The bedroom needn't be completely devoid of clutter, but any mess should be kept to a minimum and never overtake the room. A bedroom space should also feature only necessary furniture. The bed is the focal point of any bedroom; any additional space around the bed can be left open for "breathing" space, or bring in select pieces of furniture to promote relaxation, such as a chaise longue.

A Perfectly Imperfect Bed

A comfortable bed with quality bedding is the most important element of a bedroom from a design perspective, as well as a practical one. The bed takes up the most space and is therefore the centerpiece of the bedroom; the eye naturally goes to this piece of furniture, so it should be attractive. However, the comfort of the bed is paramount. Given how much time is spent asleep and how crucial quality of sleep is to our overall health and well-being, the mattress and bedding must be cozy and conducive to rest.

Your personal preferences (and perhaps those of your partner), your budget, and the size and look of your space will guide your choice of bed frame. You may prefer the solidity of a sturdy wooden frame, the classic look of iron, or the softness of an upholstered headboard. This piece of furniture is an investment and likely something you will live with for a long while, so it is worth taking time with your choice.

While less expensive than the bed frame, bedding is still an investment. Again, consider your personal aesthetic preferences as well as what feels good against your skin. Do you like the texture of linen or cool, crisp cotton? Do you prefer the weight and warmth of a down comforter or the nostalgia evoked by a hand-stitched quilt?

I adore a perfectly imperfect bed, a made but slightly disheveled look that beckons me at the end of a long day (or for a mid-afternoon nap!). I don't want to remove stacks of matching throw pillows or untuck hospital corners before diving under the covers. My perfect bed is covered by a soft gray, crinkly linen duvet atop simple, soft white cotton sheets. A few slouchy pillows against the headboard are ready for me to lean against when I read before bed, and a throw blanket tossed along the foot of the bed is on hand for a cat nap or an extra layer on a chilly evening.

61

Soft Colors and Textures

Are there certain colors that relax you? Do you find peace surrounded by white walls, or do darker rooms make you feel calm and cozy? Now think of textures that bring you comfort. For you, is there nothing quite like sinking into a deep leather armchair, or do you love the feeling of a freshly laundered pillowcase beneath your cheek?

To create a calming, relaxing environment, I incorporate peaceful colors and soft textures throughout our bedroom. Soft, earthy colors in shades of gray, beige, and pale blue are throughout the space, from the walls to the floors to the bedding. Large, fluffy sheepskins mark the floor on either side of the bed, making our first and last steps of each day gentle and sweet.

Lighting

The lighting in the bedroom is one of the most impactful design decisions to create a calming environment. Proper lighting will set the mood, whether you're up and starting your day or settling in for the evening. An overhead light is ideal for moments of cleaning, organization, and getting ready for the day. For the evening hours, however, consider using dimly lit bedside lamps or sconces. The soft lighting will help to prepare your body for a night of sleep.

Koen and I love to light bedside candles as we prepare for bed. We allow the flames to flicker as we find

our pajamas, brush our teeth, climb into bed, and read. When it comes time to turn out the lights, blowing out a candle is the most peaceful feeling, a gentle cue for our bodies that it is time for sleep.

When the lights are out for the evening, the bedroom should ideally be pitch black, with no glow from electronics or from the outside world. If you live in a city and lights filter into your bedroom at night, consider hanging dark curtains.

MOMENTS
TO UNWIND

I find it nearly impossible to hop into bed, close my eyes and immediately drift off to sleep, even though that is precisely what my body so desires. More often than not, I mentally replay the happenings of the day, run through my to-do list, or think about the next day's schedule. Before I can fall asleep, I need time to unwind and relax my mind. To settle my mind, I write my thoughts in a small journal that lives on my bedside table, a natural sleep aid. Sometimes, I jot a list; other times I scratch a random string of unrelated thoughts. The act of writing allows me to release my thoughts rather than leaving them to race through my mind. I find that reading has a similar effect. However, my bedside books differ from those found in the living room. I purposefully choose gentle books on topics that are easy and pleasant, and not unsettling.

Create the Moment
What relaxes you? What is your bedtime routine, and how does it help you to wind down from the day so that you are ready for a night of rest? As you prepare for bed, avoid activities that cause stimulation or stress. Try to dedicate the hour before bedtime to preparations for sleep; this gives your body time to enter a state of relaxation and for your mind to shed the cares of the day.

Design the Moment
My bedside table and the things that rest on top are aesthetically pleasing, but everything serves an important purpose and helps me to get the rest that I need. As you arrange your bedside table, consider items that encourage slumber. An attractive bedside lamp anchors the things on the night table; a light bulb with low wattage offers enough light to read and to make you feel sleepy. A small alarm clock allows you to leave your smartphone in another room entirely. A simple candle lends a feeling of coziness; a journal or book can help you to quiet your mind.

A PLACE OF REFUGE & COMFORT

I was a typical teenager, a happy girl busy with school work, activities, and friends. One of my lasting memories of those years, though, was how much I loved coming home at the end of the day. Most evenings, my mom would prepare dinner for my dad, my sister, and me. I would walk in the door, slip off my shoes, put my backpack down, and breathe the scent of home—and whatever was on the stove. It was this moment when I knew that the hardest part of my day was over. My mother would treat our family to a comforting meal and I could relax and be myself.

I'm fortunate to have similar experiences in my adult life. My husband, Koen, loves to cook, and some evenings I will arrive home after him, opening the door to be greeted by candlelight, the sound of music, an amazing aroma, and the sure knowledge that I am home. I think of entering my home almost as receiving a hug—my home is pulling me in close, welcoming me.

Home is where we find the most comfort. We can let down our guards and relax. Of course, it is possible to find comfort outside of the home—in your favorite coffee house or bookstore, for example—but your home belongs to you alone. It's a retreat from everything else in life, a place for just you and those you hold dearest.

LIVING SPACES

I laugh just a bit when I think of the living rooms in the homes of some of my friends' parents growing up. They were in big, suburban homes with formal living rooms: white wall-to-wall carpet, pristine furniture, and a firm "do not enter" policy. These were showrooms—there was no "living" done in them. Many American homes today still maintain both a family room or den as well as a more formal space. If you are among those who have multiple communal spaces in your home, I encourage you to use the "formal" space, too. After all, what are you saving it for? Perhaps this space simply becomes a quiet room, a space to read quietly or to enjoy moments of solitude. The family room or den may continue as your primary "together" space. Whatever type of space you have, try to imagine how to use it in a way that best suits you and your loved ones and how you live.

The living room is a place to be at ease and enjoy being in the moment. It may be a place for lounging, for conversation—lively or intimate—for reading, playing games, or watching a movie. In many homes, it is where people choose to spend the most time. Although larger living spaces allow for entire families to come together (or for great parties to be thrown!), it can be a challenge to create a sense of intimacy. In large living rooms, the space can be made to feel cozy if it is separated into two or more distinct areas; take advantage of the extra space and design for two or more types of "moments." Smaller living rooms are lovely in that they have an inherent coziness. It is far easier to design and arrange a room to cultivate a feeling of togetherness: sofas and chairs are grouped closely, and so, naturally, are the people who spend time there.

A well-considered living space design—no matter how large or small the room—takes into account the various activities that might take place there. The design should allow for these activities and encourage moments of comfort.

Seating

Comfort and good design are not mutually exclusive when it comes to sofas and chairs, thankfully. This linen sofa has a cozy, lived-in look that unpretentiously lures people in and the soft texture of the sheepskin draped on the back adds an extra level of comfort.

71

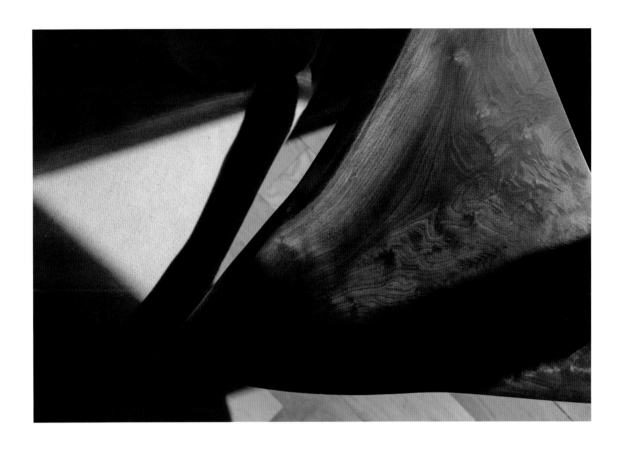

Accent Tables

Accent tables in the living room should be selected with available space and purpose in mind. In a small living room, a narrow, oval coffee table offers a place to put up your feet or to stack an assortment of attractive coffee table books while minimizing the risk of bumping your shin as you pass through the room. A side table at just the right height placed perfectly beside a comfortable chair is just the spot to rest a book or a glass of wine and will quickly become a coveted spot.

Lighting for Mood

Take care with the lighting in your living room, as good lighting is a key element for creating a comfortable environment. An overhead light may give the entire room a glow but consider adding standing lamps in the corners and table lamps near seating areas. Scatter candles around the room for coziness. Proper lighting will add ambiance, and with an endless array of shapes and sizes, each can be a design statement of its own.

Don't be afraid to experiment with lighting. Move lamps around the room until the lighting feels balanced in the space. Or, embrace different lighting combinations for different moods and situations. If we are having friends over for a game night, we might light only a few table lamps for a cozy atmosphere, just enough light to see the game board. If we are trying to wind down before bed, we may light candles and a single dimmed floor lamp.

Decorate for Comfort

Soft textures and textiles immediately cozy up a room. We keep a basket of blankets of varying weights, textures, and origins near our sofa— lightweight cotton throws for summer evenings when the sun goes down, and thick, woolen blankets for our cold mountain winter nights. These are beautiful, and they remind us of special moments and people in our lives. Some we collected on our travels; one is a vintage find from my favorite weekly market in Amsterdam, and another was made by a dear friend.

An array of pillows in different shapes and sizes elevates the design of a room. You can mix and match, swapping pillows with the seasons or to find the perfect one for a Sunday afternoon nap.

Wood, leather, sheepskins, brick and stone, and organic textiles are timeless and soothing, and they wear well, improving and acquiring character with age.

Natural Materials

Natural materials are particularly well-suited for living rooms. Wood, leather, sheepskins, brick and stone, and organic textiles are timeless and soothing, and they wear well, improving and acquiring character with age. Earthy colors and textures help to create a feeling of calm and offer an excellent design base to which you can add artwork, books, and other home décor items for personal flair.

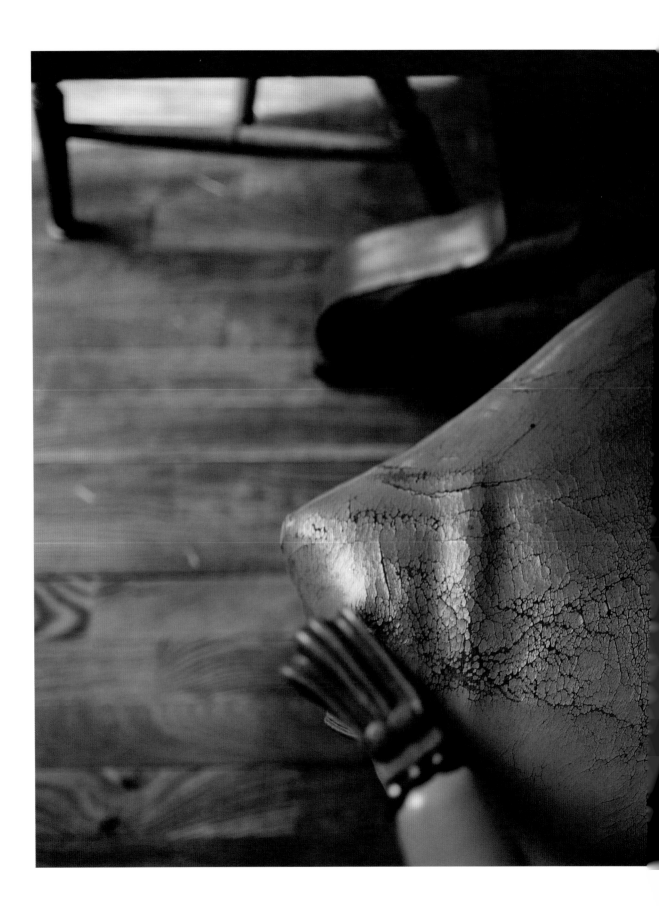

MOMENTS
OF COZINESS

Koen and I live in a neighborhood nestled in a valley between two ski resorts in Colorado. The winter is filled with snowy, cold days with plenty of sunshine. We ski often; our proximity to the mountains is one of the reasons we choose to live where we do. The skiing itself brings us joy, but the moments after a day on the slopes are when we experience the real hygge. I love walking into a warm restaurant or pub at the end of a ski day. I rest my legs, sip a hot drink, and feel my body slowly warm by the fire, luxuriating in what is, for me, the ultimate moment of coziness. In fact, Koen and I embrace time spent fireside all winter long. We build fires nearly every night during the cold months. We love the warmth and cozy ambiance; we get the fire going as soon as we get home in the evening, enjoy it as we cook dinner, and even occasionally pull a small table to the hearth for a fireside meal.

Create the Moment
Even if you don't like cold weather, it's impossible to deny that there is nothing like a chilly day to make you want to reach for your favorite sweater or throw blanket and snuggle in. Make your plans for a cozy night in the next time a storm is brewing; gather your loved ones close and play a board game or enjoy an indoor picnic fireside. Let the rain or snow come down as you cozy up next to a roaring fire or a hot stove.

Design the Moment
A fireplace or wood stove is often the focal point of the room it is in. How might you arrange furnishings to emphasize this feature and maximize opportunities for coziness? In this home, a rocking chair and a leather chair and ottoman are pulled close to the stove, beckoning you to sit and warm your feet. Wood is stacked nearby, ready to feed the fire. Interesting books, unique artwork, and even an unusual axe give character and depth to the space.

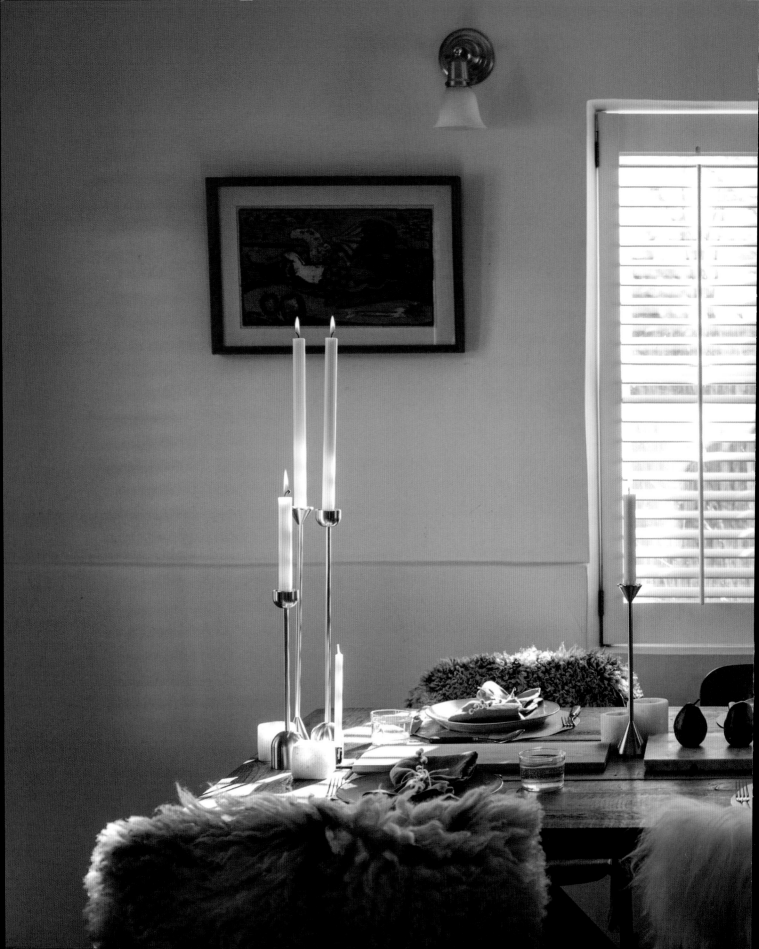

GATHER

GATHER

GATHER

Create spaces to enjoy time with the people you cherish.

DURING the years I lived in Amsterdam, Koen and I had regular dinners with his family at his parents' home. I vividly recall feeling as if the evening would never end during the first few meals I shared with them. We ate course after course and drank multiple bottles of wine. Conversation was drawn out, and just when I thought we must be almost finished, there were still rounds of espresso left to be had. The food was always delicious, the wine divine, and the conversation enjoyable, but I would leave completely exhausted and overwhelmed by the formalities—and by the endless conversation. I remember asking Koen how his family could possibly talk as much as they did! They also seemed preoccupied with table manners, embracing formal customs like keeping hands above the table at all times and always using the proper cutlery. At first, I didn't understand the rules, but as an American guest at a European dining table, I tried my best to mimic what everyone else was doing. Over time, what I came to realize was that my experience wasn't unique to my time with Koen's family. The Dutch culture strongly values deep, thoughtful connection, and they dedicate much time and energy to nourishing their most treasured relationships.

At home in the United States with my family, dinners are much more relaxed. Everyone sits around the table and is involved in the conversation, but there are no real formalities and the meal is typically a single course, occasionally followed by dessert. We laugh and enjoy a feeling of ease and comfortable connection, but the meal may only last an hour or so.

After experiencing and dissecting dining practices from both cultures, I have learned to appreciate both types of gatherings. I now have the fortitude and stamina for a European dining marathon and can keep pace with the courses and conversation. I have learned to set my mind to a long, indulgent evening, and these are some of my most treasured times with Koen's family. I also appreciate the relaxed, homey feeling of dining with my family here in America when we gather to enjoy each other's company and worry less about the formalities.

Life's most precious moments are spent in the company of people you cherish. Most will readily agree that life is richer and more fulfilling when it is shared; a number of studies show that deep, meaningful connections with others make us happier people. In your own home, you can thoughtfully design spaces to encourage opportunities to gather and facilitate moments of connection with family, friends, and neighbors.

Life's most precious moments are spent in the company of people you cherish...life is richer and more fulfilling when it is shared with others.

A WARM WELCOME

My sister lives with her husband and their three children in a charming brick bungalow in an older Denver neighborhood. I love to stroll around her neighborhood. Each house has its own unique characteristics: some have brightly colored doors, others have deep front porches. During the holidays, beautiful wreaths adorn the doors and carefully strung lights give a warm glow. Cozy coffee shops and cafés intersperse the quiet residential area.

One fall afternoon, we sat on my sister's front porch, enjoying a glass of wine and a warm chimenea fire, watching the kids run around and chase insects. As the afternoon turned to evening, neighbors passed by on the sidewalk, pushing strollers or walking their dogs, always stopping to say hello. There was so much activity and life in these moments; without any effort at all, I was enveloped into their community, their conversations, the loveliness of their everyday life. I felt at home and welcome, connected to my sister and her family in a simple yet profound way. I recognized how their front porch living set the stage for these varied interactions, and that there is an art to greeting guests warmly and generously.

There is an art to greeting guests warmly and generously.

THE ENTRANCE

Each time we welcome guests, I hope they experience a similar feeling of warmth in our home. Your guests' impression of your home begins as they approach the front door. When we are expecting company, we like to light a special outdoor candle (one that won't blow out in the wind) that glows deeply and brightly, a simple gesture to demonstrate that we are anticipating our guests' arrival with pleasure. A wreath on the door and a brightly lit entryway similarly convey a cheerful greeting.

The welcome you extend to the inside of your home begins in the entry. A thoughtful approach to both the function and aesthetics of the entryway is necessary to convey a warm welcome; after all, this is where your home offers its first impression and where the tone is set for the time you will spend with your guests. Just as importantly, it is your point of departure and entry each day. Think for a moment of how you feel when you walk in your own front door. Do you experience that embrace—that feeling of welcome? Do your guests?

The most basic function of the entryway is obvious: it is how one enters (and leaves) the home. Because it's so seemingly straightforward, it can be easy to neglect this space,

but it plays an important role. It's where you don your coat and shoes and prepare for the responsibilities that the day will bring. It's also where, at the end of the day, you transition from your many roles in the outside world to a place where you get to simply be yourself. When you consider this, the entryway is so much more than a portal through which you enter and leave your home. Rather, it's a place where you mark important transitions in your daily life. As such, the design of this space deserves thought and attention. However basic, including the following elements in your entryway both make your home feel welcoming and provides simple ways to enhance your daily life.

A Place for Everything

The entryway is a natural catch-all space for all kinds of items. The items that you take with you in the morning and bring home with you in the evening land in the entryway. To keep this area organized—and a pleasant area to pass through—make sure that there is a place for everything (and everything in its place). A beautiful bowl or decorative box can hold keys, mail, or a cell phone. Pegs or a coat rack are an easy place to stash a jacket or a handbag. If you have a dog, the entryway is an ideal place to store a leash, treats in a jar, or even the water bowl for easy access.

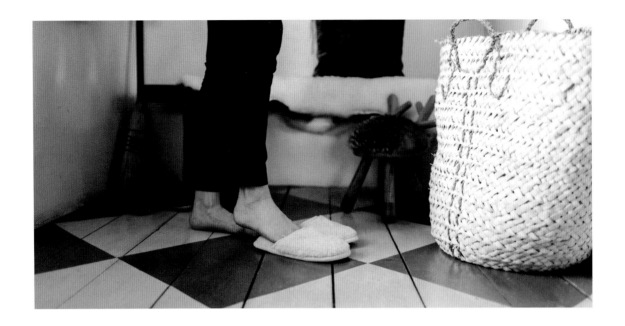

Slippers

In Japanese homes, you will often be
greeted by a rack of slippers in all
different sizes. We have adopted this
tradition: we like to keep an attractive
basket filled with comfortable woolen
slippers for guest use near our front
door, a way to ease their transition
into our home and to make sure
they are comfortable during their
time with us. Since we live in the
mountains where the evenings tend
to be chilly, even in the summer,
this gesture is appreciated. We find
that our friends let their guards
down and feel at ease as they divest
themselves of their street shoes. We
keep our own slippers by the door as
well.

SINCE 1906

Personalize Your Entryway Space

While the entryway is a practical space, that doesn't mean you shouldn't seize the opportunity to have some fun with the décor! In fact, personalizing your entryway—even striving to make it funky and unexpected—has the potential to be a great icebreaker for guests and to set the tone for a fun get together!

Come old friends
Drive up in state
A welcome extends
Both early and late

MOMENTS
OF GREETING

Throughout my life, whenever I visited my grandmother's home, she always offered me a cup of tea immediately upon my arrival. I thought this behavior was unique to my grandmother, but when I lived in Europe, I recognized that this was a common gesture of hospitality. I learned to accept a beverage whether I was thirsty or not, because the acceptance was as much a part of the custom as the offer. To accept the drink was to allow the host to welcome me into his or her space; it marked the beginning of our time together. As the teacup or wine glass passed from the host's hands to my own, I found that anything I was doing or thinking beforehand would evaporate and I would find myself present and ready to enter into a new moment of connection.

Create the Moment
Consider offering a welcome drink whenever you have guests in your home, a small but meaningful gesture to convey how happy you are to be in their company. If you are entertaining in the winter, a big pot of mulled cider on the stovetop lures people with its enticing aroma.

Design the Moment
Elevate the moment and make your gesture of hospitality even more special by serving a beverage (in accompanying glassware) to suit the season, the occasion, or even the feeling you want to create. A lovely Sauvignon Blanc served in a delicate, vintage etched floral wine glass is perfect for a springtime brunch, or a sturdy, chilled mug of beer is ideal for a backyard barbecue.

AT THE TABLE

As our business, *Hygge Life*, evolved from a blog to a home décor shop (and now with a café), Koen and I craved a more personal way to share hygge with others. We began to host *Hygge Dinners*, special ticketed events where we intentionally created a hyggelig atmosphere and experience. We select settings for these dinners that are unusual, but always warm and conducive to an intimate dining experience. We have hosted dinners at a family farm, at a historic warehouse, and even in a home that was once a church. We go to great lengths to style the dining table at these events to foster connection. All guests gather at one long table adorned with charming, mismatched blue and white dishes, dozens of candles, fresh flowers, and handwritten menus. The flicker of the candles sets the mood for the evening, and the seats and benches are softened with cozy sheepskins to provide comfort and encourage our guests to fully relax as they dine.

The food is prepared by incredible chefs and often cooked over an open fire in front of our guests. The crackle of the fire, the sight of the fresh ingredients, and the aroma of the cooking connects people to the food they are about to enjoy.

During the dinner, these fire-cooked dishes are served family-style—our favorite way to dine. The passing of platters and the serving of food acts as a natural ice-breaker; friends and strangers alike interact as they fill their plates. As people dine, Koen and I do a bit of storytelling, sharing about the meaning of hygge and the art of creating cozy moments around the table and at home. We relish these intimate evenings and believe that they truly bring hygge and happiness to people's lives. Our hope is always that the people who gather around the table will carry their experience with them and strive to recreate it with their own families and friends.

DINING SPACE

The dining table—whether found in a formal dining room or a cozy kitchen nook—is where we find nourishment. It is where we spend time each day to fuel our bodies, where we break bread together, feeding ourselves both literally and also in how we find togetherness and a sense of community. Koen and I love to spend time together with our family and friends, as most people do, and we find that our most enjoyable times together usually take place inside a home, gathered around a table. When we bring guests to the table in our own home, we strive to incorporate many of the elements from our Hygge Table dinners. Whether it's your immediate family gathering for a weeknight meal or a larger gathering of extended friends and family, it is surely worthwhile to make your dining space comfortable and inviting, conducive to enjoying the time spent with one another. Such a space gently encourages those gathered to be present in the moment, focused on each other, engaged in sharing their thoughts through conversation.

Newer homes may embrace open concept living with a dining area that flows with the kitchen and living spaces. Some homes may feature both a formal dining room table and a more casual table in the kitchen area. Different types of dining spaces are conducive to different types of moments. In homes that do have a formal space, that room may be used rarely; the kitchen table may be the go-to gathering place for most meals. Rather than adhering to convention and maintaining a seldom-used formal space, instead focus on creating spaces that you will actually use. Often, this doesn't require purchasing new furniture or redoing the space, but rather reframing how you think of the space. For example, a formal dining room could be reimagined as a cheerful breakfast room, a place to read the newspaper and enjoy a leisurely cup of coffee. Or, if you find that you often host large groups of people, simple changes in décor, such as surrounding the table with an array of comfortable chairs or benches, may transform the room into a space where people naturally gather. If your kitchen table gets wonderful afternoon sunshine, make a point to pause together here for a cup of tea in the late afternoon before jumping into your evening routine. Think of moments like these that have the power to enhance your life and strengthen your connections with those you love and optimize your dining space to facilitate these special times.

A Breakfast Nook

In the morning, as we wake up for the day, we crave a more intimate, soft space. A breakfast nook tucked in the corner with a comfortable bench or sheepskin covered chairs lit by a candle or soft overhead lighting provides a perfect space to ease into the day. Consider finding a spot in your kitchen or dining area that gets morning light or simply feels cozy and make this a morning coffee and breakfast nook. Place a small table here to fit a cup of coffee, tea and a breakfast plate, along with a few comfortable chairs or a built-in bench. Set a single taper candle on the table for a gentle morning glow and drape a sheepskin on each chair, or at least on the seat you sit in most.

A Special Table

This walnut dining table and chairs are more special then most; they are designed by the renowned George Nakashima whose pieces are coveted by design lovers from around the world. Here, the table is placed prominently by a wall of windows, illuminating its beauty and giving the dining set the attention it deserves. Although the table spans the width of the room, the design is airy and organic; it doesn't overwhelm the space but seems to float in the room gracefully. This dining table seats eight and is suitable for formal dining occasions but is also a place to read the newspaper in the morning as sunlight pours through the windows. While not in use, this extraordinary piece remains a focal point in the home.

A Thoughtful Table Setting

While Koen loves to cook, my favorite part of preparing for a meal is setting the table. I relish creating an atmosphere suitable for the type of food that will be served, who will be sitting around the table, and the occasion or season. We have a tucked-away kitchen cabinet filled with tablecloths, napkins, candleholders, antique silver spoons, cheese knives, and so on. Our collection continues to grow as we fall in love with special pieces on our travels, items almost always found while perusing flea market stands or shopping in small, local boutiques. While certain items—like Koen's grandmother's crystal champagne coupes—are kept for truly special celebrations, I try to use the items in this cabinet as often as possible, even when it's just a weeknight meal with the two of us. The table isn't decked out with décor for every meal but taking the time to intentionally create an atmosphere is incredibly satisfying, even if for a casual home meal where everyone fills a big ceramic bowl with a hearty soup from the stove and sits around the table lit with a single candle, sharing a bottle of red wine.

Comfortable Seating

Seating around the dining table should be comfortable enough to allow for long conversations and lingering at the table. Chairs needn't be upholstered to be comfortable, in fact, bench seating naturally creates a feeling of togetherness and is an easy way to make a table feel cozier.

Whether a table has chairs or benches, we often like to drape sheepskins on our seating. The padding and softness increase the cozy factor even more and add a feeling of casual luxury.

Linens

Dining tables are made to be used, and as such, they are *not* meant to be pristine. Scratches and nicks appear over time and add character to the furniture. Likewise, table linens eventually show wear, but I argue that this simply adds to the charm. Think of colorful, quality French table linens that fade with washing and drying in the sunshine. What could be lovelier? Likewise, Belgian linen tablecloths and linen napkins needn't be perfectly pressed. In fact, the nature of linen is such that gentle wrinkles are part of the very look of the fabric. Linen washes easily and only gets better with use. Embrace these "imperfections" and let them be subtle reminders of the good times you enjoy around your table.

Durable Dishes

While I adore the look of vintage china and the stories that come along with them, I find that I prefer to use sturdy, durable dishes. I know that these pieces can handle almost anything with grace, from rowdy dinners with my nieces and nephews to backyard barbecues to a holiday meal. The same is true for glassware; in fact, jelly jar glasses have an inherent charm and are nearly indestructible. Functional yet beautiful tableware will withstand the test of time and allow you to relax and let life happen around your table, with worries about broken dishes far from your mind.

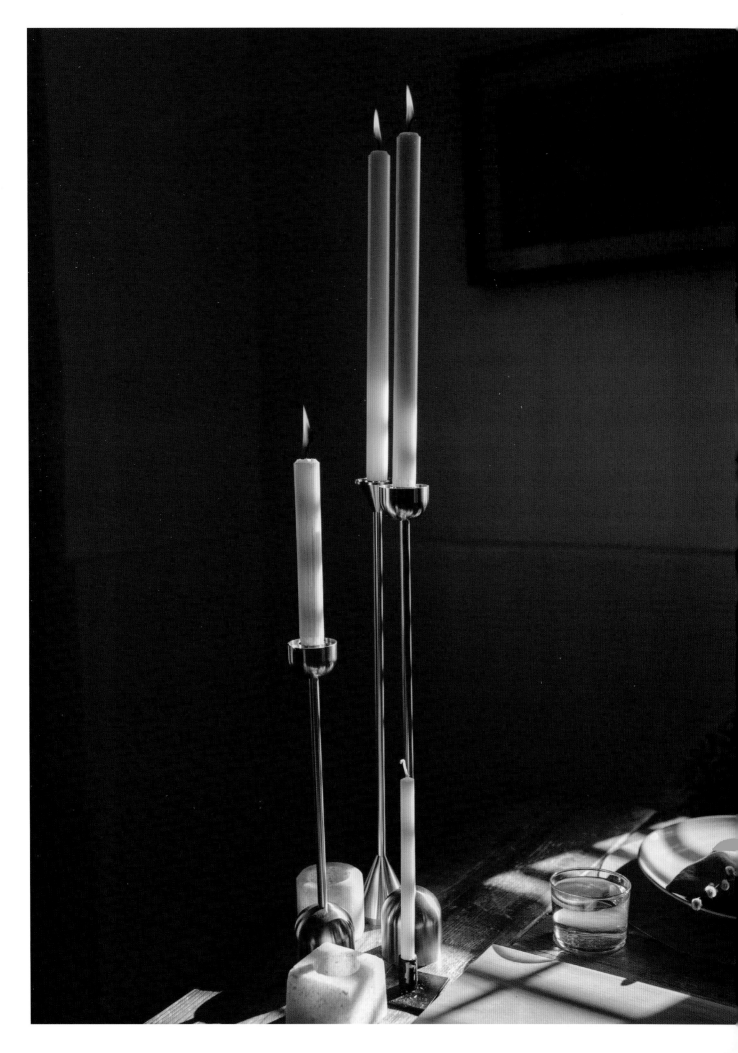

Lighting

As with every space in the home, the proper lighting is a crucial element of a comfortable dining atmosphere. Overhead lighting fixtures come in an array of styles, giving you endless décor options from rustic to industrial, classic to modern, and everything in-between. It's lovely to have overhead lighting on a dimmer to create a more intimate feeling in the space.

For us, the best dining table lighting is candlelight. In our home, a meal doesn't go by without a candle lit. Our table invariably features some combination of taper candles, pillar candles, or even tealights in tiny holders. Lighting a candle marks a moment—it means that you will be there, in that particular space, for a length of time. This acknowledgment prompts you to slow down and enjoy that time. We find that the act of lighting a candle helps us to release any preoccupations and let go of distractions and focus on enjoying a meal together.

MOMENTS
OF EVERYDAY CELEBRATION

A long, lingering lunch is a French tradition, and our dear friends from France host a community lunch every Sunday, bringing guests around their table each week with grace and pleasure. They hang a sweet chalkboard in their window that says, "S'il vous plaît joindre à nous pour le déjeuner du dimanche. Tout le monde est le bienvenu." which translates to "Please join us for Sunday lunch. Everyone is welcome." This brings neighbors, friends and family around their table for a leisurely, indulgent Sunday meal. Children play outside in the courtyard while their parents enjoy nice conversation. The table is filled with freshly baked bread, hard boiled eggs, gentle cheeses, jellies, and an array of sliced meats from the butcher, and of course, bottles of wine. It is simple and unpretentious, and a lovely way to connect with a different group of people each week. The Swedes also have charming traditions for getting together. On Friday evenings, they come together for "Fredagsmys" to celebrate the end of the work week with food and drinks. Everyone brings a dish or two, and friends enjoy a relaxed time together—and sometimes enjoy the host's sauna. Swedish people are also known for fika, a word that translates to sharing coffee with others. These coffee dates are marked by their intimacy, a way to share quality time together.

Create the Moment

Friendly get-togethers like these are lovely opportunities to gather people around your table. You might embrace these traditions or adapt them to suit an American way of life, such as a barbecue with horseshoes or backyard volleyball. Seek creative opportunities to bring people together for casual gatherings. If you don't entertain often, this may seem daunting at first, but you simply need to flex your hosting muscles. After a few get-togethers, you will learn to be at ease and enjoy the moments that unfold!

Design the Moment

Whatever opportunity presents itself, be thoughtful about the gathering. Small details make for big aesthetic impact. Light candles, adorn the table with flowers, and use cloth napkins. If you decide to host a brunch, serve fresh croissants from a local bakery in a beautiful basket or perhaps offer a special drink, like a rose latte in a glass mug. A dinner might feature deep, generous bowls of warm butternut squash soup or a delicious, fresh salad paired with a glass of crisp white wine, depending on the season. Attention to décor as appropriate for the event shows that you have put effort and thought toward creating an enjoyable occasion, small gestures which in turn demonstrates your regard and affection for your guests.

AROROUND THE HEARTH

Somewhere in Spain, not too far from Barcelona, Koen and I became stranded in the Hygge Bus camper van after the gearbox malfunctioned. Fortunately, we were near an off ramp and could exit the highway safely; unfortunately, it was a Sunday. The Spanish garages weren't open for business and we were forced to park in the lot of an abandoned bodega. Luckily, the camper was our home that summer, so we didn't have to arrange a place to stay, but our journey was unexpectedly halted and our surroundings for the evening less than ideal. The camper van had a double bed in the back, a small kitchen with a sink, stove top, and a few cabinets along with two upholstered bench seats with a table in between. It had everything we needed, but it was small and cramped. We were cozy, to say the least. Stuck in the camper with nowhere to go, we laughed about our situation and made the best of it. As it turned out, this unforeseen stop was one of our favorite moments from the trip and became a memory we carry with us. We couldn't run the car and we didn't have electricity, but we did have candles. We prepared a simple pasta supper, drank a bottle of wine, and played cards by candlelight. I remember laughing for hours, having so much fun together in our tiny home on wheels. There was nowhere else to be and only so much we could do, so we simply enjoyed each other's company that night in the camper.

Since ancient times, people have drawn together for warmth and connection. We feel this same pull in modern times. While we might not always gather around a fire as our ancestors did, we still crave being physically together with others, engaged in conversation.

Since ancient times, people have drawn together for warmth and connection. We feel this same pull in modern times.

Intentionally create a home environment that encourages gathering for moments of togetherness...

While it is fulfilling to be with friends in our homes, home is also the place where inhabitants interact with one another each and every day, waking each morning and going to sleep each night, enjoying meals, and relaxing together. Home is where our deepest connections are fostered and where our most precious moments occur. With a thoughtful approach to home design and décor, we can actively, intentionally create a home environment that encourages gathering for moments of togetherness and allowing ourselves to be vulnerable and true with one another, a sure way to cultivate rich connections with the people you hold dearest.

135

GATHERING SPACES

When you entertain, in what spaces do people naturally congregate? When it's just your family, where do you tend to spend time together? Are these rooms thoughtfully arranged to make conversations feel easy and natural?

Conversational Seating

What is the most coveted seat in your house? Do you have a particularly well-worn, comfortable chair that people rush to claim? Or, do you have sofas or chairs that feel awkwardly placed? Living room seating should be arranged to bring people together to relax and connect with one another. Sofas should face each other; chairs should be drawn close together. Does the television occupy the center of attention in the room? You might consider making conversation the focus of the room, with the television placed less prominently in the space. Consider who uses your living room, but also how the space is used, and arrange your seating accordingly. It's okay to play with furniture arrangements until you achieve the look—and more important—the feeling that you want.

Casual Connection

There are also areas in the home that may facilitate casual conversations, an easy-going, everyday togetherness. A bar top can be a great place for pleasant chats with family members or guests. Instead of shooing people from the kitchen as you prepare a meal, an open countertop or island is a natural gathering place where everyone feels comfortable and at home. You might even put those who stray into the kitchen to work chopping vegetables or pouring wine!

MOMENTS
OF EASY JOY

We have good friends with whom we enjoy themed dinners. We alternate hosting duties, and the cuisine, drinks, and table setting are all part of the experience. So far, we have had Japanese, Italian, Dutch, and French-style dinners. On Japanese night, we drank delicious sake and ate with chopsticks from bowls that our friends brought back from their recent visit to Japan. We heard interesting stories of their travel adventures (and misadventures!) and laughed all night long. On another evening in our home, we cooked a hearty, traditional Dutch meal that began with homemade fries and a citrus flavored mayonnaise for dipping. Koen loved being able to share his culture through food and the fries were delicious! It's exciting to give these dinners a theme; this naturally prompts different topics of conversation and much more laughter than a usual dinner gathering. These dinners linger in our memories and smiles linger on our lips long after the evening is over.

Create the Moment
Strive for a playful home! Gathering with others is not always about deep conversation or formal dinner parties. Low-key get-togethers—whether with your partner, your immediate family, or with friends—can simply be fun! There is so much pleasure to be found in an evening of laughter and jokes in a casual setting. It's important to let yourself go, to not take life too seriously, and to enjoy relaxed, joyful connection with others. Of course, you don't need an "event" for time together. It's just as important to slow down and connect with your immediate family. Designate a weekly hygge night: this could be pizza and a movie on Friday night, or pajamas and board games on Sunday evening as a way to end the weekend. Cater these evenings to what your family likes to do but try to make whatever you choose a regular occurrence. The healthy anticipation of this time spent together will add to the joy.

Design the Moment
Keep a basket or drawer of games easily accessible. In our home, we take this one step further and keep a set of dominoes on the coffee table! Break out a deck of cards or a board game on a weeknight as a way to disconnect from the work day and transition to a state of relaxation and enjoyment. We also find that games make for an easy transition from the dining table to the living room when we have friends over for dinner. This change of activity and scenery allows for a different type of connection, including more laughter, easy conversation, and fun.

BE

BE

BE

Create spaces to encourage intention and contentment in your daily life.

WHILE living in the Netherlands, I visited a dear friend to meet her newborn baby. We sat in her living room where two deep, comfortable couches faced each other, a coffee table placed in between. Her new baby boy was nestled on a soft, shorn sheepskin, cozy and content. I cuddled up next to the baby while my friend made tea, and we shared the afternoon, speaking in hushed tones and adoring her sweet baby. Of course, there is nothing like welcoming a beloved new baby to bring you into the present moment. The precious new life commands attention and awe. That afternoon, there was simply nowhere else to be and nothing else to think about other than this new little person and his mother. It is precisely because I was so wrapped up in the moment that I remember this day so fondly, years later. Our friendship grew strong and our bond deepened through our shared experience that day.

Imagine if we could experience all of life's moments with this level of intensity and presence of mind. While that's likely not possible, we do each have the capacity to be more present and intentional in our daily lives. Culturally, most of us are conditioned to constantly think about our endless to-do lists, to obsess over what's next, to chase after goals. However, we cut ourselves short when we don't allow ourselves time to truly just *be*. Think for a moment about the last cup of coffee you drank. What did you do as you sipped the coffee? Did you scroll through your phone? Or, did you truly enjoy that warm drink in that particular moment? It's true that it's just how it goes sometimes, but it's also true that these moments of mindlessness accumulate—quickly— and many of us might look back over the last day or week—or even years— and realize how little time we truly enjoyed and fully lived.

It's these fully lived moments—no matter how inconsequential—that can make life more meaningful and enjoyable. Look for opportunities to be present, to eliminate petty distractions and grant your undivided attention to the moment you're in. Believe it or not, your approach to the design of your home can influence—positively or negatively—your ability to slow down and simply *be*.

*Look for
opportunities
to be present, to
eliminate petty
distractions
and grant your
undivided
attention to
the moment
you're in.*

CARE FOR YOURSELF

My best days begin with quiet, peaceful moments when I allow the time to slowly awaken. I wake and stretch luxuriously before I roll to the edge of my bed. As I place my feet on the ground, I relish the feeling of the soft sheepskin on my toes—an especially welcome sensation on chilly mornings. From here, I make my way to a corner in our bedroom where I keep a basket that holds a yoga mat and stretching bands, along with a small table that holds a single candle. I love to take a few moments to stretch or for a slow yoga routine, followed by a moment of meditation to center myself for the day. For me, having this corner set and ready for my ideal morning routine makes it more likely that I will actually engage in this activity.

We can't give what we don't have, so goes the adage. We must take care of ourselves if we are to be able to truly connect with ourselves and with others. Likewise, it is extremely difficult to feel fully present in a moment while feeling unhealthy or unhappy. To live intentionally and with contentment begins with proper self-care. Think of your home as a sanctuary, a place where you can create a personalized retreat, a peaceful haven.

THE BATHROOM

Have you ever walked into a gorgeous bathroom and sighed with pleasure? I have had this experience a few times and I always take note of the elements that create this atmosphere. Often there is natural light coming from a window or skylight. The surfaces are largely uncluttered, the towels thick and soft, and even the scent of the hand soap is lovely. Sometimes a stay in a beautiful hotel will reveal just how lovely a bathroom space—complete with monogrammed fluffy white bathrobes—can be.

While a bathroom serves everyday practical hygiene needs, a thoughtfully designed space can bring indulgent, pleasurable moments to your daily self-care routines. It is a place to pamper yourself. "Pampering" may be as simple as washing your hands with soap in your favorite scent or it may be a long, candlelit bubble bath at the end of a long day. In this small space, careful attention to a few key elements will make the bathroom a place where you can truly indulge and renew.

155

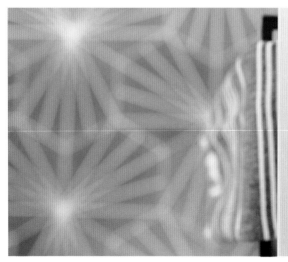
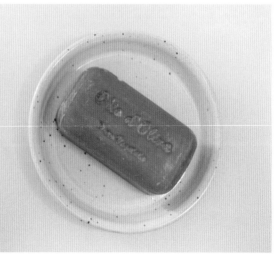

Towels

Quality cotton or linen flat weave towels are beautiful hung or draped in the bathroom. In the winter, you may consider a thicker terry towel for extra comfort.

Quality Bath Products

Use quality, natural bath products that feel good on your body and are also pleasing to the eye.

Natural Elements

Bring greenery into your bathroom for a feeling of freshness, like a sprig of eucalyptus in the shower that gives off a serene scent when caught in the steam.

A Tidy Space

Keep the bathroom counters free of clutter to put your mind at ease and allow for serene moments.

Small Room, Big Personality

A bathroom can be peacefully neutral or full of personality. Vibrant colors and bold patterns in wallpaper, tile, and even fixtures make these rooms unexpected and joyful spaces.

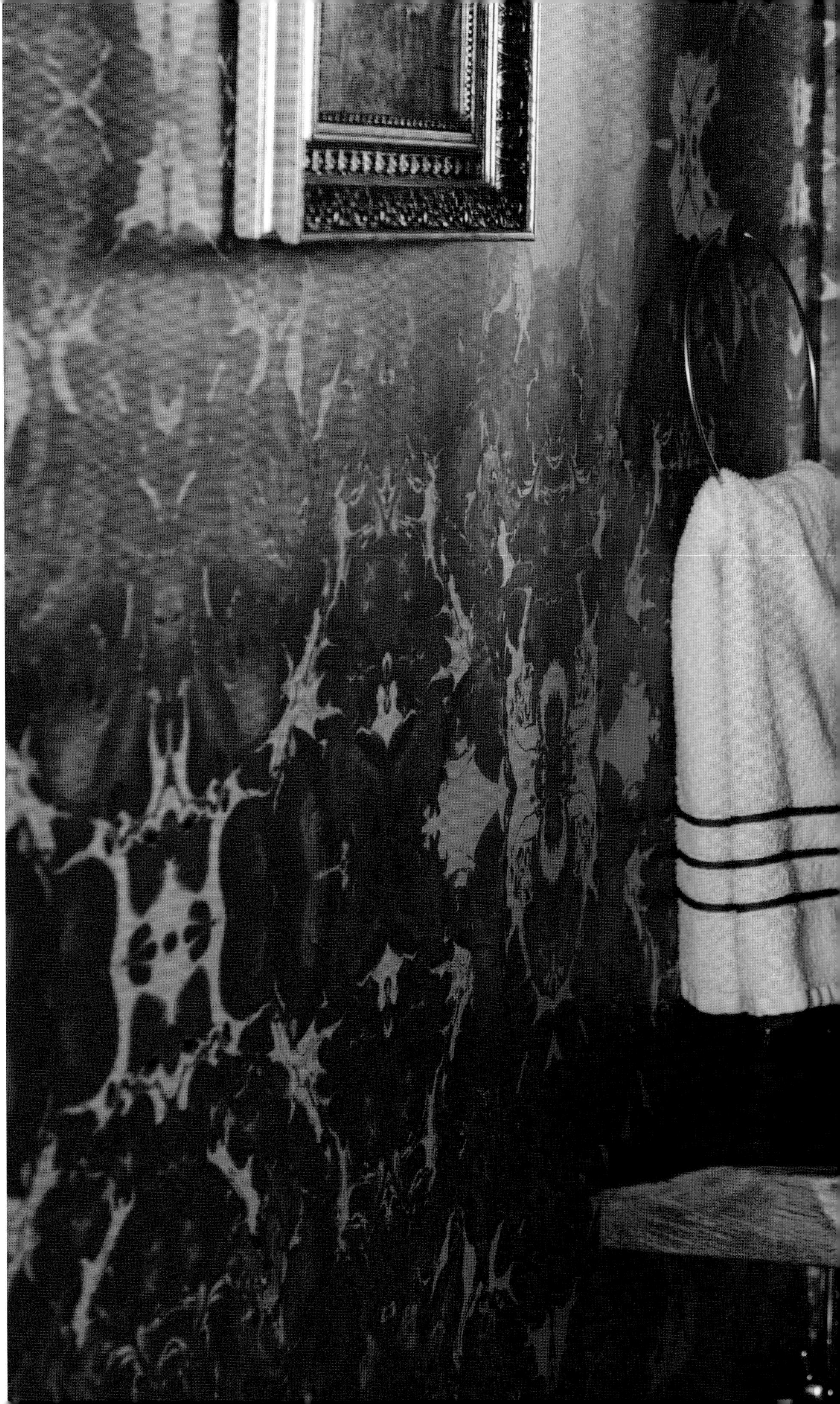

CREATE A SANCTUARY

Your home is your haven, your sanctuary, a retreat from the rest of the world. You are careful with *who* you allow in your home; be equally thoughtful about *what* you allow in.

Your home is your haven, your sanctuary, a retreat from the rest of the world.

Keep Tabs on Technology

I recently stopped at a favorite local café. I had carved the time out of my afternoon—an hour to myself to be out of my house and away from the shop, a single hour to enjoy a cup of coffee and a bit of relative quiet. I left my phone in my car, however, I was startled by how uncomfortable and self-conscious I felt as I sat there alone. Even though I knew I didn't have my phone, I kept patting my pocket—physically reaching for a device to scroll through.

It can be uncomfortable to be the sole person staring into space in a public place. However, home is the ideal place to disconnect from devices and connect, to allow yourself to be present in the moment. Consider adding elements to your home to help you keep technology use in check. Koen's family used to place their phones in a basket during the dinner hour; and now phones at the table are strictly taboo. This is a good first step, but you may choose to take things a bit further. For example, establish a table near your entryway where you can plug in your device as you arrive home and leave it there for the evening. Shed your digital distractions so that you can relax and be present at home, focused on time to be quiet and unwind or to connect with family members. Give yourself—and your loved ones—this gift of time away from technology.

While technology can create barriers between people, a television can also arguably bring people together; I know many young families that love to enjoy weekend family movie nights. However, consider for a moment how much of our lives—and our furniture arrangements—are centered around the television. I've been in many living rooms and felt like something was off and then realized that all of the seating was awkwardly arranged to face the television screen, often making it

difficult to face other people to have a conversation. If you have multiple living spaces in your home, consider keeping the television tucked in a side room that isn't the main living area. If you have one primary living space, consider the other activities that take place in the room and tuck the television to the side or in a cabinet with doors so that it doesn't steal the show, so to speak.

Breathe Deeply

Fresh air and natural light do
wonders for your state of mind
and should be brought into the
house whenever possible. Open
the curtains—and the windows—
and breathe the fresh air deeply.
If you live in a sunny climate and
the sunlight is too intense, sheer
lightweight curtains can help to
diffuse light as it filters into your
home. In gray, rainy climates, the
soft light naturally creates a hyggelig
atmosphere. In northern Europe
where gray days are the norm, people
leave the curtains pulled and shades
up all day to soak up as much light
as possible and seize the opportunity
to light candles, even during the
daytime.

Bring Nature Indoors

Home is where we shelter against the outdoors, but there are simple ways to bring nature inside. Natural, organic elements have a soothing effect and offer endless options for simple, inexpensive pieces that add a sense of life to your home. Potted herbs like basil, thyme, rosemary, and mint are at home on a kitchen windowsill and add fragrance to the air and flavor to the dishes you cook. Houseplants brighten and add cheer to any room, and many even improve the air inside your home.

Sheepskins and textiles made from natural materials like cotton or wool add layers of coziness; furniture made of wood is durable and lends a space a sense of solidity and permanence. We like to keep a large stack of wood beside the fireplace in our living room. Each piece of wood is different than the next and the overall effect is not unlike an intentional art installation. Likewise, interesting pieces of driftwood act as sculptural *objets d'art* for shelves or tables.

Outdoor Living

If you have outdoor space surrounding your home, make use of this
space as a natural extension of your
indoor living area. Time spent
in nature has a direct, positive
impact on health and happiness.
Read a book on your front porch
and enjoy a gentle breeze. Grow a
kitchen garden and create an easy
source of fresh ingredients to add to
your meals. Chickens in a backyard
coop will provide beautiful, speckled
eggs to brighten your mornings.

*Time spent in
nature has a
direct, positive
impact on
health and
happiness.*

MOMENTS
OF SOLITUDE

As the owner of a bustling retail shop, I interact with people all day, every day, both in person and via the telephone, email, and social media. I truly love these interactions and I'm thankful that they are a part of my daily life. I get to collaborate with wonderfully creative people from all walks of life, not to mention, of course, the customers who visit our store. Many of these people are repeat customers; others I meet for the first time as they pass through town. Either way, I treasure the opportunities to connect and share hygge. While I thrive on these interactions, I also require time spent in solitude and quiet each day, crucial to my ability to recharge and to be my best self. Time where I can read, or simply gaze out the window, thinking about anything or nothing at all.

Create the Moment

In a world full of people to meet and places to go, strive to designate spaces in your home that encourage time to slow down and just be—spaces for quiet moments. A Danish hyggekrog is a cozy place to curl up, a small place where you feel safe, warm, and content. You may drink tea or read a book—whatever activity makes you feel at ease.

Design the Moment

Most living rooms—even small rooms—will have a place where you can carve out a quiet nook. You may choose a space with a view out of the window or a corner near the fireplace. We love the hyggekrog in our living room, a place where either of us can sit alone in addition to a more conversational seating area where we spend time together or with friends. In fact, it's ideal when these two arrangements—a cozy nook and conversational seating—can coexist in the same space. After all, sometimes it's lovely to feel together, even when you want a moment of quiet to yourself.

The most crucial element of a hyggekrog is a comfortable place to sit, a lovely chair or a deep window seat. Place a small table nearby to rest a book, a candle, and a mug or wine glass. Throw a warm, soft blanket over the arm of the chair; add a throw pillow or two if you'd like. Arrange a lamp with soft lighting nearby for the evening hours.

Children love to have their own space, too. My sister and I were the queens of making forts when we were children. We loved making little nooks in our bedroom, places where we would retreat to read or play or just feel cozy. Create a kids' hyggekrog in their bedroom or even in the living room. This can be as simple as a corner with big, fluffy pillows and a few toys or books, or a more elaborate indoor teepee or fort.

SEEK EVERYDAY JOY

One of my daily pleasures is walking into the kitchen early each morning. I open the curtains and sunlight pours through the kitchen windows. I love to see how the light changes day to day, season to season. Sometimes the anticipation of this simple ritual is what gets me out of bed in the morning. Once the curtains are open, I make my way to our coffee nook, a corner where we keep all that we need to make a warm beverage: our espresso machine and tea kettle, a coffee grinder, our favorite ceramic mugs, and heavy brass spoons for stirring in honey or scooping frothed milk. We take our time as we make our morning coffee, the process as much a part of the experience as the drinking. We love to make a pour over coffee for the first cup of the day; certainly, this takes more time than an automatic machine set to brew just as our alarm rings, but from the intense aroma of the coffee beans being ground to watching the steam billow as water is poured, I believe that it adds more hygge and enjoyment to the experience. We light a stout, unscented "breakfast candle," a perfect accompaniment for quiet morning moments, as part of our morning coffee ritual, and in this way, we mark the beginning of the morning with calm and togetherness before the busyness of the day sets in.

EMBRACE RITUALS

Not every moment is idyllic and peaceful. Our daily lives are filled with responsibilities, like household chores. Although it may sound silly, choosing to be present in the midst of even mundane activities can make these moments more fulfilling. While a shift begins with your mindset, thoughtful design can go a long way to infuse a bit of the extraordinary into otherwise ordinary, monotonous tasks.

Dishes

For years, washing dishes was my most dreaded daily task. All I wanted to do was relax, and instead faced a stack of dirty dishes, a smelly sponge, and the daunting prospect of spending the next thirty minutes standing at the sink. One day, I splurged on a few beautiful wooden dish scrubbers. I brought my purchases home and gave them a place in a pretty ceramic container. That evening, I found an unexpected sense of satisfaction—even enjoyment—as I washed the dishes with my new finds. Over time, I have continued to use similar tools; I have also made it a practice to reflect on the meal I just enjoyed with a sense of gratitude as I scrub and rinse. Over time, I have extended this philosophy to many otherwise onerous chores. I seek beautiful, finely crafted tools and enjoy using them for whatever task is at hand.

Making the Bed

While I might not love making my bed each morning, I *do* love the small jolt of happiness I get whenever I pass through my bedroom during the day and see the neatly made bed. Knowing this, I embrace the few moments it takes to make my bed in the morning as a moment of transition into my day, a way to ease from rest to productive, waking hours. I straighten our heavy comforter, plump the lovely throw pillows—pausing to enjoy these beautiful items that we so carefully selected—and go about my morning. And when bedtime comes each evening, I relish peeling back the sheets and crawling under the covers.

It is unrealistic to think of life as a string of highs. In fact, life is largely small "in-between" moments (and is punctuated with some lows, too). All of these moments—the good and the bad—combine to make up our lives, and none should be discounted or ignored. Sometimes, we coast through the in-between times in anticipation of the next exciting event, a habit that may cause us to inadvertently rob the current moment of its potential for joy. If this is true for you, shift your habits and observe the small, seemingly meaningless moments of transition in daily life. Look for joy in these small moments and make the everyday feel special.

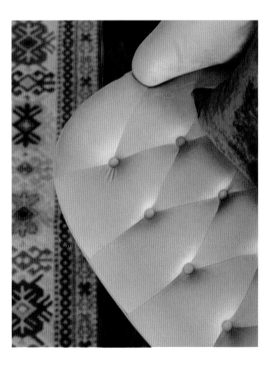

184

I have a friend who started a cocktail blog. Born out of her passion for spirits and travel, she writes about tequila toddies, Icelandic martinis, and Japanese whiskeys, among others. She stocks an impressive home bar and has a fantastic imagination; on Friday evenings in the summertime, we love to stop by for a specially prepared surprise drink. As much as I enjoy that first refreshing sip, I also love seeing the care and creativity that goes into its preparation. Something as simple as a cocktail feels somehow momentous, and it's a perfect way to end the work week and ease into the weekend enjoying a delicious drink amongst friends.

PURSUE HOBBIES

My mother loves giving gifts. Not only does she have a knack for selecting thoughtful, meaningful gifts that are perfect for the recipient, she also takes great joy in beautifully wrapping packages to make them even more special. She has a wrapping table with an enormous collection of pretty ribbons, bows, and paper. A huge cork board hangs on the wall behind her table; here she tacks bits of inspiration: postcards from her travels, magazine clippings, and even swatches of fabric and ribbon.

Koen's mother is a bookbinder. She owns several big, heavy machines, including an antique book press and a traditional embosser. She keeps a large paper cabinet to store materials and papers that she's collected from around the world. Now that her children are grown, she has two entire rooms in her home dedicated to her craft.

Each of these women have dedicated space in their homes to pursuits that bring them joy. Not everyone can dedicate entire rooms as my mother-in-law has done, but each one of us can design our homes in ways that reflect our interests and passions and encourage us to pursue them.

Dedicate space in your home to the activities you enjoy.

Music

Dedicate space in your home to the activities you enjoy. This living room is home to a beautiful piano and guitar, treasures belonging to a musician in the family.

188

Artist's Corner

The nook in the back of this study fills with afternoon light, an ideal artist's retreat tucked away in a quiet corner.

Writing Table

Instead of a computer station, consider tucking an elegant writing table into a quiet corner of your home, a nod to less technologically-focused times. Place a supply of your favorite pens in a jar; stock the desk with a beautiful journal or quality stationery. Keep a box of notecards ready for thank-you notes, or occasional messages to loved ones. Keep the décor around the desk simple—a favorite piece of artwork, a pretty houseplant, and an unusual table lamp create a striking visual vignette. I have found that having a place like this to retreat makes me more likely to spend time recording my thoughts in a journal or writing a note (and less likely to scroll on my phone).

NINE STORIES · J.D. SALINGER

EDGAR ALLAN POE

the Count of Monte Cristo · Alexandre Dumas

VICTOR HUGO Les Misérables

CAMUS THE STRANGER

JANE EYRE Charlotte Brontë

The Pelican Shakespeare · The Taming of the Shrew

DAHL Matilda

WILDE · THE PICTURE OF DORIAN GRAY

EXTREMELY LOUD & INCREDIBLY CLOSE
JONATHAN SAFRAN FOER

PLAYED WITH FIRE · STIEG LARSSON

Ian McEwan On Chesil Beach

Warm Springs SUSAN RICHARDS SHREVE

The Guernsey Literary and Potato Peel Pie Society
MARY ANN SHAFFER AND ANNIE BARROWS

ALICE SEBOLD

MICHAEL CHABON
THE AMAZING ADVENTURES OF KAVALIER & CLAY

BROTHERS K DAVID JAMES DUNCAN

AYN RAND ATLAS SHRUGGED

STORY Robert McKee

DONNA TARTT The Goldfinch

One fish two fish red fish blue fish Dr. Seuss

THE SANDMAN — dream country NEIL GAIMAN
THE SANDMAN season of mists NEIL GAIMAN

the ONION AD NAUSEAM

the ONION Platinum Prestige Encore Gold Premium Collector's Collection

The Far Side GALLERY 4 Larson

See inside Space

MAKE WAY FOR DUCKLINGS by Robert McCloskey VIKING

THE ILLUSTRATED ENCYCLOPEDIA OF DOG BREEDS JOAN PALMER

Larson The Pre-History of THE FAR SIDE

DAVID FOSTER WALLACE Infinite Jest

MIDDL

Reading

If you love to read and to surround
yourself with books, line your most
precious titles in large wooden
bookcases. For an unpretentious,
relaxed vibe, simply stack unusual
or compelling titles along the wall.

MOMENTS
OF PAUSE

Our days are spent juggling; there are endless tasks as we tend to our brick and mortar and online stores, plan our Hygge Table dinners, and carve out time to spend with family and friends. Our lives are rich, but also busy; if we allowed it, Koen and I could be pulled by the weight of our responsibilities from the moment we open our eyes in the morning until we collapse into bed each night. To live this way is inherently problematic: we become slaves to routine, driven to always do more, and we go through the motions without ever fully processing the moments that make up our lives. Rather than falling victim to these external forces, Koen and I try to hold each other accountable to intentionally carve moments each day to pause and simply breathe. I so often feel that I will never accomplish all that I set out to do in a day. It can be easy to sit down at my computer in the morning and when lunchtime comes, I find that I've barely looked away from the screen. It can feel difficult to justify taking a break, but when I do pause in the middle of the day, it ends up being even more rewarding than anticipated.

Create the Moment
When can you find time to pause during your day? Whether it's ducking around the corner for a mid-afternoon cup of tea at a café near your office, taking a brisk walk in a local park, or even luxuriating in a Sunday afternoon nap, try to find a window of time each day to stretch your legs, take a deep breath, and do something enjoyable.

Design the Moment
The views from our kitchen are stunning; when the afternoons slow down, Koen and I sometimes sneak away from the shop to sit at the table in the sunshine and look at the mountain vista while sipping on a cup of tea and enjoying a light snack. The sunlight, the cozy table, the rustic teapot, and the mugs that fit perfectly in our hands—the combined effect of these small pleasures is a perfect respite from the busyness of the rest of the day.

A REFLECTION OF YOU

We have friends in the Vail Valley who are true mountain lovers, avid skiers and mountain bikers who live for the outdoors. When we visit and walk up the steps leading to their home, there is gear on the patio and in the entryway: in the summertime, bikes are parked just outside and ready to be ridden and the barbecue is uncovered and put to daily use. In the winter, skis hang on brackets in the entryway and ski boots are drying by the fire. The walls of their house are adorned with framed trail maps and a painting of the local Gore mountain range. While their home is where they recuperate from their outdoor pursuits, it is also a place that clearly reveals their passions and priorities. Their home is a true reflection of all that they hold dear.

On the other side of the ocean, other friends own a floristry in the middle of bustling Amsterdam. They have built their love of flowers, plants, and all things green into a thriving business. Walking into their home is like walking into a dreamy greenhouse. A large indoor tree occupies a corner, blooming branches are scattered around the home and bouquets of all types sit upon any available surface. Their love of fresh, vibrant florals is evident from the moment the door opens. Even their beautiful son reveals their love of flowers with his charming name, Floriën.

Each of these homes is unique and full of personality, true reflections of those who live inside them. After all, a home doesn't exist only to help us meet our basic needs or to give us a place to gather. At its best, home is also a place that is intimate, personal, and true to *you*. Whether you rent or own, in your home you have the opportunity to create and design a space to cultivate the experiences, feelings, and moments that make your life enjoyable and meaningful. Your home evolves until it is a reflection of you—and what could be more beautiful than that?

Home is a place that is intimate, personal, and true to you.

CATER TO YOUR INTERESTS
AND PASSIONS

Your interests and passions should be reflected in your home—not only in the way it looks, but also in the way you live inside it. Does your family enjoy playing games together around the coffee table? Do you like movies and pizza every Friday night? Do you like to enjoy a glass of wine with your partner at the end of a work day?

It's essential to reflect on the way you live before you seek outside inspiration. Rather than picking a room layout from a design magazine or blog, truly take a moment to examine your space and consider how you and your family use it. Likewise, pause to think of what truly makes you feel both grounded and joyful. Is it a treasured photograph or a piece of furniture you inherited? If it's important to you, find a place for that object in your home. The pieces you love will come together to create a thoughtful, hygge home.

It's essential to reflect on the way you live before you seek outside inspiration.

Meaningful Objects
Incorporate furniture and objects that are meaningful to you and tell a story. This ornate antique bird sconce was inherited from a relative; the artwork adorning the stairwell was collected on distant travels.

Books

Books are the ultimate functional décor. In all sizes and colors and covering any topic imaginable, books look beautiful when styled on shelves with other objects, set atop a coffee table, or even stacked on the floor. I love to visit other people's homes and browse their bookshelves. I learn so much about my friends' interests simply by observing what they read.

Photographs and Artwork

Personalize your home by framing photographs of your most treasured people and memories or hanging artwork that you love.

203

Reflect Everyone

An abode that is home to multiple people should likewise reflect the tastes of each person who lives in the home. This includes children! If you have children, look for ways to incorporate the things that interest them in areas throughout the home. Here, a tiny, low shelf is tucked beneath the windowsill, perfect for the young children in the home to access their favorite stories.

MOMENTS
OF PLEASANT IMPERFECTION

My grandparents were passionate antique collectors; they traveled to Europe often to collect beautiful pieces to sell in their shop. Of course, they kept many special pieces: paintings, armoires, leather chairs, and decorative objects. The aging leather, wood, and varnishes create a bouquet of worldly wisdom; the scent of an antique store still makes me feel like a young girl, running from room to room to explore the countless treasures that fill my grandparent's home. When I was young and first living on my own, I once asked my grandmother how I should choose furniture for my home—how I should figure out what my "style" was. Her advice was simple: "Choose pieces that you love, and they will naturally come together to make a beautiful home." In other words, there was no need to chase trends or to adhere to a certain design style or color palette. Only by being true to myself would I be able to create an abode that feels like "home." Over the years, I have realized time and again the wisdom in her words, and its advice I am always pleased to share with others.

Create the Moment

Release any expectation you may have that you can create a "perfect" home. It's silly to put this pressure on yourself. More often than not, it's the personal details—the imperfections that show our home is lived in—that make it truly comfortable. Beneath the desire to be perfect is perhaps a reluctance to be vulnerable. While it may be tempting to strive for perfection, instead allow the look and feel of your home to reveal the real you.

Design the Moment

Although I love the calm that I feel when my house is tidy, I also find comfort in having my favorite things at hand. To me, a bit of a mess can be charming, even comforting. Have you ever been a guest in a home where absolutely nothing is out of place? It can be a bit intimidating; it may even inhibit your ability to connect—after all, who identifies with perfect? It's perfectly alright to stash your favorite sneakers within reach, to pile magazines and newspapers near your reading chair, or to leave a jigsaw puzzle half-finished on the coffee table. Become comfortable with the evidence of daily activity; this demonstrates that your home is alive, in use, and beloved.

A FRAME FOR LIFE   ILSE
                      CRAWFORD

CONCLUSION

HOME is where you are nourished—body, and also spirit. It is where you find rest and rejuvenation. It is where you seek and find comfort, where you gather with loved ones, and where you are able to simply be yourself. Home is where our values, interests, and tastes are rooted and grow, where you are the fullest expression of yourself.

Home is so much more than a simple shelter; it is where you flourish. Each home is unique to the person who dwells within; it needn't be a magazine-worthy space, but it should reflect you and the life you want to live. Design elements combine to create a space that meets your needs and is aesthetically pleasing, but most importantly, a space that helps to cultivate meaningful moments that enrich your life.

RESOURCES & INSPIRATION

THE FOLLOWING BRANDS—and the people behind them—are sources of hygge inspiration. Some of their products can be seen in the pages of this book and in our shop. Their stories are dear to my heart.

ATELIER SUKHA

Sukha means 'joy of life' in Sanskrit, and that is exactly how you feel when you walk in the door of this lovely Amsterdam shop. The owners, Sam and Irene, believe in sustainable production and take great care in creating unique items from natural materials. All of their products are handmade by women's fair-trade empowerment groups in Nepal and India.

WWW.SUKHA.NL

NEW COLLAR GOODS

Jon and Deana are the husband and wife team behind this Denver, Colorado woodworking studio. Not only do they make beautiful furniture, we are lucky to consider them our good friends. Deana, a talented cook, prepared the elaborate feast seen in the book.

WWW.NEWCOLLARGOODS.COM

SIROCCO LIVING

A collection of Danish- designed products that bring hygge and warmth to any interior. All products are made with natural materials by artisans in Egypt using traditional handcraft techniques. Their beautiful products have a Scandinavian look with Sahara flair.

WWW.SIROCCOLIVING.COM

HUNT MODERN

A design gallery located in the high desert of Santa Fe, New Mexico. The owners, Brad and Lauren, collect furniture from around the world, with a focus on European design of the 20th century. Their timeless home is featured throughout the book.

WWW.HUNTMODERN.COM

ELDVARM

These Swedish-designed fireplace tools and accessories are exquisitely made, the perfect accents for cozy fireside moments.

WWW.ELDVARM.COM

EDIE URE PILLOWS

Each of Edie's plant-dyed velvet pillows is unique in its coloring and intensity due to the natural dying process. Our favorite fact: the pink pillow is dyed with avocado pits!

UASHMAMA

These versatile and washable paper bags and natural home accessories are made in Tuscany by the lovely Marconi family. Their dream is to open a workplace retreat in Tuscany where children are welcome and daily meals are shared around the table.

WWW.UASHMAMA.COM

BROADWICK FIBERS

Camille, owner of Broadwick Fibers, hand dyes and felts raw wool into yarn and then knits luxurious blankets and wall hangings.

WWW.BROADWICKFIBERS.COM

EO

Tor and Nicole started EO with a passion for designing products with clean, simple lines and a vibrant, original flair. They collaborate with designers from around the world to create products with universal appeal, like the iconic Bambi Chair.

WWW.EO.DK

FS OBJECTS

A home goods product line designed and manufactured in Brooklyn. Using natural materials, their designs are rooted in simplicity and functionality.

WWW.FSOBJECTS.COM

213

HOMES

THE VARIOUS homes that we visited and photographed during the creation of this book all speak to me in different ways. Some have "high design" elements that reflect the passions of their owners. Some have a soothing, minimalist vibe, while others show rich layers of family history and memories. Despite their differences—or perhaps because of them—the design of each home feels intentional. Each is a place where I felt welcome, delighted by the moments I spent there. And of course, that is what *Dwell, Gather, Be* is about.

SHAKER-INSPIRED
The longtime dream of designers Kim and Marke Johnson, this shaker-inspired home has a unique mix of materials, colors, and personality. It is completely original and full of character, just like their design company, *The Made Shop*. The couples' design office is next door and separated from their Denver, Colorado home by a grassy courtyard.

WWW.MADESHOP.COM

MILSTON WELL FARM

Milston Well Farm, a family farm full of character, charming details, and family heritage, is home to Margaret & Chris Schutze and their two young boys, Miller and Houston. Together, Margaret, an interior designer and Chris, a carpenter, have created a dreamy family home and farm with goats, donkeys, chickens, and an enviable garden. They have two Airbnb homes on their property and host a handful of weddings each year.

WWW.MILSTONWELLFARM.COM

COZY ADOBE

Our first shoot took place in a cozy adobe home on a hilltop in Santa Fe, New Mexico. The bedrooms, kitchen, and living room open to a sunny courtyard and views of the Sangre de Cristo mountains. Each room is intimate, warm, and full of character.

HUNT MODERN HOME

Owners Brad and Lauren have a passion for modern design and living well. Their home and business, Hunt Modern design gallery, are both located in the high desert of Santa Fe. They collect furniture from around the world, with a focus on European design of the 20th century. Their home is filled with many of these lovely collected pieces, reflecting their lifestyle and love for timeless modernism.

WWW.HUNTMODERN.COM

MOUNTAIN MODERN

This thoughtfully designed mountain home is fresh and modern, with warm natural wooden details and exposed ceiling beams. The large windows and doorways in each room frame breathtaking mountain views and let in plenty of sunlight. Located just a few blocks from downtown Boulder, Colorado, this home has the feel of a mountain retreat.

THANK YOU

WRITING *Dwell, Gather, Be* was a pursuit filled with moments of eye-opening reflection and wonderful collaboration. This experience would not have been possible without the help of many people along the way to whom I am incredibly grateful.

Thank you to Blue Star Press for providing this opportunity and for your generous support along the way. I respect and admire the time, energy, and passion that you put into your projects. It has been an absolute pleasure working with all of you. I am especially thankful for the unending support of my editor and publisher, Alicia Brady. She truly lives a hygge life and is reflected on these pages as much as I am. I can genuinely say that we have become friends through this project and I will miss our weekly conversations.

Thank you to Ali Vagnini for beautifully capturing the spaces and moments featured throughout the book. Her photography is genuine and full of life, just like she is. It was truly special sharing this experience with you, Ali.

Thank you, Lauren and Brad, Margaret and Chris, and Kim and Marke for inspiring me and welcoming me into your lovely homes. The moments captured inside your spaces give life to the words I have written and are a testament to the thoughtful homes you have created.

Thank you to all who contributed to the creation of this book or offered encouragement and inspiration. My sincere hope is that those who read these pages will be inspired to design their home around the moments that they treasure.

And lastly but definitely not least, thank you to Koen, my husband, for his support, love, and encouragement over the past two years. There were many long days and busy months when I needed extra support in order to fulfill this dream and Koen was always there to offer his helping hand.

ABOUT THE PHOTOGRAPHER

ALI VAGNINI lives in the Rocky Mountains of Colorado and works both locally and worldwide. Her imagery reflects a passion for telling honest stories which allows Ali to capture any client's true spirit. Ali fuels her own spirit by spending time in the mountains with her partner Matt and her fur-child Hank.

ABOUT THE AUTHOR

ALEXANDRA GOVE is the owner of *Hygge Life*, a lifestyle brand and Scandinavian-inspired home décor shop just west of Vail, Colorado. After living in Amsterdam and traveling around Europe for several years with her Dutch husband, she was inspired to bring hygge back to her home in the US. Alexandra was a hygge pioneer, bringing this Scandinavian lifestyle to the US in 2013, before the trend swept the country. She has a passion for interior design and creating a life and home with thought and intention. Alexandra and her husband, Koen, run their brick & mortar shop, café, and online store together. They also host a "Hygge Dinner" series where they gather people around the dining table for good food, drinks, connection, and an overall hyggelig experience. They dream of opening a small hotel where they can continue to share this cozy, intentional lifestyle. *Hygge Life* has been featured in *The New York Times*, *Dwell,* and *Real Simple*, on Colorado Public Radio, and in the award-winning *Finding Hygge* documentary film, among other publications.